Bottles, Cans, Plastic Bags

Written by Roderick Hunt and Annemarie Young

Illustrated by Alex Brychta

OXFORD
UNIVERSITY PRESS

The family was camping at the
seaside. Dad was painting something.
"What are you doing?" asked Mum.

"I'm painting this empty snail shell purple," said Dad. "It's for a game to play on the beach."

Later on, Wilf and Wilma arrived
with their parents.

"We saved the spot next to us for
your tent," said Dad.

"Thanks," said Wilma's dad. The family started unpacking and began to settle in.

"This will be fun," said Kipper.

"I'll cook a barbecue for us all," said Wilma's dad.

"Thanks," said Mum. "We can go and explore the beach."

Waste &
Recycling
Point

"I'll get rid of this rubbish," said
Dad. "They have good recycling
bins here. There's even one for
food waste."

The beach was in a sandy cove.
There were rocks to climb, rock
pools to look in and a cave to
explore.

While the children were paddling in the sea, Dad hid his purple snail shell among the rocks.

"Sometimes, a rare shell can be found here," said Dad. "It's the purple sea snail. It's really lucky to find it."

"I'll give a prize to anyone who finds one," he said.

The children raced off to search for a purple shell.

Wilf, Biff and Kipper searched
along the shore line.

"Ugh!" said Kipper. "Look at all
these plastic bottles."

Chip and Wilma searched among
the rocks and rock pools.

"All this litter!" said Chip. "I can
see two plastic bags in this pool."

Suddenly, something moved
behind a rock. A seagull was tangled
in the plastic rings from some drink
cans, so it couldn't fly.

Dad held the gull carefully in his
sweater and Mum untangled it. The
gull hopped and then flew away.

"Why do people leave litter on beaches?" said Wilma. "Look at the harm it can do to wildlife!"

The children collected as much
litter as they could. Wilma's mum
got something to put it in.

"We're learning about recycling at school," said Biff. "Cans can be recycled, and paper can be recycled up to six times!"

"Do you know that duvet filling can be made from recycled plastic bottles?" said Wilf. "So we could be sleeping under plastic bottles!"

"Well," said Dad. "The beach is much cleaner now, thanks to you. Let's wash our hands, then see who can find a purple sea snail!"

"There are bits of broken purple shell by this rock," said Mum.

Oh no! Someone had trodden on Dad's shell by mistake.

When they got back, Wilf's dad
had made a delicious barbecue.

"There won't be much leftover food
to recycle," said Wilf.

"Sleep well," said Dad. "It's been a busy day."

"We never did find the purple sea snail," said Chip, with a yawn.

Mum went to bed but Dad stayed outside. He had a little job to do.

"Bedtime," Mum called, softly.

"I won't be long," whispered Dad.

Talk about the story

Why did Dad paint a snail shell?

What did the children do with the litter they found on the beach?

How did Wilma feel when they found the seagull?

What do you recycle at home?

Sort the rubbish

Which recycling bins would you put these things into?

Which of these things can you find in the pictures of the story?

Snail trail maze

Help Kipper find the purple sea snail.